To

From

Date

Raising Up a Little Girl

PAINTINGS BY

Sandra Kuck

HARVEST HOUSE PUBLISHERS

EUGENE, OREGON

RAISING UP A LITTLE GIRL

Art copyright © by Sandra Kuck

Text by Janna Walkup, copyright © 2011 by Harvest House Publishers

Published by Harvest House Publishers

Eugene, Oregon 97402

www.harvesthousepublishers.com

Design and production by Garborg Design Works, Savage, Minnesota

ISBN 978-0-7369-3850-1

Scripture quotations are taken from the New King James Version. Copyright © 1982 by Thomas Nelson, Inc. Used by permission. All rights reserved.

Harvest House Publishers has made every effort to trace the ownership of all poems and quotes. In the event of a question arising from the use of a poem or quote, we regret any error made and will be pleased to make the necessary correction in future editions of the book.

Printed in China

11 12 13 14 15 16 17 18 / IM / 10 9 8 7 6 5 4 3 2 1

CONTENTS

She's Waiting for You!

Through the activities of their days and the charms of their personalities, little girls give us frequent and entertaining glimpses of what they may become. We can just see...

- the caring mother who lovingly nurtures her baby dolls.
- the delightful diva with a style all her own—courtesy of the dress-up box and vintage jewelry from Grandma.
- the determined young artist who creates a construction paper-and-crayon masterpiece.

These babes in our arms and hearts quickly become girls with their own personalities, preferences, and unique ways of doing things. As mothers, great-grandmothers, grandmothers, aunts, and family friends, we're privileged to provide the loving guidance steeped in caring that girls need to become all God created them to be.

Girlhood is a time of friendship and fun, delight and discovery, imagination and emerging independence. You've been entrusted with the task of raising—or helping to raise—a little girl. You have the worthiest task of all—to prayerfully help her develop a heart of beauty, a character strong and true, and a presence filled with loving grace. And you'll experience many, many joys and wonders along the way!

The attributes of a great girl may still be found in the rule of the four S's: Sincerity, Simplicity, Sympathy, and Serenity.

EMILY POST

Just remaining
quietly in the
presence of God,
listening to Him,
being attentive
to Him, requires
a lot of courage
and know-how.

THOMAS MERTON

6

Raising Up a Little Girl...
to Be Courteous

He who sows courtesy reaps friendship, and he who plants kindness gathers love.

SAINT BASIL

Courtesy has become anything but common today. Yet a true Christian is always courteous, serving others before herself. She considers another's well-being before her own and gives her friends first choice. She thinks before she speaks, praying that her words will bring joy and encouragement to others.

When we raise up a little girl to be courteous, we teach her to pay attention to the needs of others and look for ways to brighten their days through the beauty around her. Consider accompanying her outdoors to pick flowers. Then you can help her arrange them in a Mason jar to brighten the breakfast table. What a delightful time of togetherness and learning that can be. Another idea is to encourage her to care for her younger siblings by entering into their world of make-believe and delighting in their favorite games, rhymes, and songs.

We *can* raise up a generation of attentive people who care enough to make courtesy common once again.

Raising Up a Little Girl...
to Be Obedient

"Why?" is quite possibly the most-uttered question by children—and oftentimes the most exasperating word to even the most patient of parents and caregivers. Yet there is beauty in this word "why":

- "Why does the world work the way it does?"
- "Why do I have to do what you tell me to do?"
- "Why can't I see God?"

These are big questions—important ones that the greatest of philosophers have asked throughout the ages. At times, though, a child's "why" is rooted in stubbornness and disobedience. There are moments in a little girl's life when she must learn to act without questioning, to obey those who have been put in charge and have her best interest at heart.

CHILDREN
ARE LIKELY
TO LIVE
UP TO
WHAT YOU
BELIEVE OF
THEM.

LADY BIRD JOHNSON

*Let thy child's first
lesson be obedience,
and the second will
be what thou will.*

BENJAMIN FRANKLIN

We encourage you to answer—or attempt to answer—her multitude of questions: "Why does the sun go to sleep at night?" "Why does the kitty purr when I pet her?" "Why does the steam rise from the soup?" Train her heart and mind to know when to question, when to obey, and when to do what is asked and ask questions later:

- We wear boots in the rain because Mommy says we must.
- We hold hands when we cross a street because Grandpa says so.
- We go to bed when it is bedtime because Daddy knows it's good for us.

In this way, you will raise a strong and secure girl full of curiosity, respect, and a heart attuned to knowing and doing what is right or best.

Faith is obedience, nothing else.

EMIL BRUNNER

To make your children
capable of honesty
is the beginning of
education.

JOHN RUSKIN

The most natural
beauty in the world
is honesty and
moral truth. For all
beauty is truth.

LORD SHAFTESBURY

Raising Up a Little Girl...
to Be Honest

Little girls love to live inside stories. "Let's pretend!" two small friends exclaim as they raid the dress-up box and pull out scarves, clip-on earrings, old prom dresses, and squares of fabric. While playing make-believe is an essential part of childhood, little ones learn important lessons as they begin to distinguish between fantasy and reality. This is an ideal time to impart the gentle lessons of truth-telling, honesty, and integrity.

Using her new paints and brushes to change the cat's hue to pink may have seemed like a harmless idea at the time, but in the face of an angry parent, a girl might be tempted to place the blame somewhere else. Yet if the little girl realizes that telling the truth is *the* most important thing—even if it means accepting subsequent consequences—she will form a character that is honest and true. Such a young girl thinks before she acts, and she will become a person of integrity who keeps her word.

HONESTY IS THE FIRST CHAPTER OF THE BOOK OF WISDOM.

THOMAS JEFFERSON

Raising Up a Little Girl...
to Be Grateful

A little girl can so easily get caught up in the flurry of unwrapping birthday presents on that most special of days: the doll she's been wishing for, an enthralling new game, that perfect pink tutu, her very first pair of ballet slippers. And then comes your gentle reminder: "Remember to say thank you!" The light in her eyes and her smile of delight show her gratitude, but the conscious act of saying "thank you" to the giver helps her develop an attitude of gratitude.

When you raise up a girl to be grateful, you raise up an individual who actively looks for the blessings in life—a breathtaking sunset, wispy cloud shapes floating across the sky, birdsongs in springtime. She appreciates the wonders of creation and the gift of companionship. A young lady who gives thanks has a beautiful heart and spirit.

Thou who
has given
so much
to me,
give one
thing
more: a
grateful
heart.

GEORGE HERBERT

Let the thankful heart sweep through the day
and, as the magnet finds the iron, so it will find,
in every hour, some heavenly blessings!

HENRY WARD BEECHER

Wake at dawn with a winged
heart and give thanks for
another day of loving.

KAHLIL GIBRAN

REJOICE ALWAYS, PRAY
CONSTANTLY, AND IN
ALL CIRCUMSTANCES
GIVE THANKS.

THE DESERT FATHERS

It is better not to say "lend." There is only giving.

PEARL S. BUCK

You can give without loving, but you cannot love without giving.

AMY CARMICHAEL

Raising Up a Little Girl...
to Be Giving

"Me first!" What a typical exclamation by children that is. Intent on their desires, focused solely on the treasure or experience at hand, it's normal and natural for little humans to want what they want *right now*. And it doesn't matter if someone else is wishing for the same thing, has the same thing, or the thing is not available. That's why such an important part of growing up is developing a spirit of giving—a Christian principle that says, "*You* can go first, *you* can choose what to play, *you* can open the present. I'll be satisfied seeing you find happiness."

What do we know about a girl who gives? She spends some of her lemonade-stand money on a toy for her baby brother. She sets aside a portion of her allowance for her Sunday school offering or gives to an organization that helps people, animals, or other causes she's interested in. She willingly helps in the house and yard, even though some of the chores aren't specifically hers. She's been taught and shown by the wise grown-ups in her life how important developing a spirit of giving is. Together they make the world a lovelier place.

Raising Up a Little Girl...
to Be Tidy

"I can't find my other shoe!"

"This puzzle is missing three pieces!"

"The dress I wanted to wear to church has mud all over it!"

So much of raising children is preparing them for the next activity—the morning trek to preschool, a visit with grandparents, playdates at the park. If a child's room—or your entire home—is a place of disorder, getting ready to go becomes a daunting task. Where are the rain boots? Where is the lunch that was packed? Has someone put the cat outside yet?

Modeling a life of order is a tremendous gift to a child. It makes her "right now" calm and peaceful. And if you help her, she'll develop the valuable skill of someday being able maintain an orderly life and home on her own. Do you know the key to tidiness? *A place for everything, and everything in its place*. Let go of perfection and focus on the *process*. Set up a few ten-minute tidies a day, and when the times come, set a clock and get started. Spend a rainy weekend helping your girl organize her room, singing songs as you work. Turn the task of tidiness into a game, and you'll nurture a love of order in your little one and a sense of calm in your household.

We put things in order—God does the rest.

HORACE MANN

The beauty of the world and the orderly arrangement of everything celestial makes us confess that there is an excellent and eternal nature, which ought to be worshipped and admired by all mankind.

CICERO

LET ALL THINGS BE DONE DECENTLY AND IN ORDER.

THE BIBLE

21

One of the secrets to a long and fruitful life is to forgive everybody everything every night before you go to bed.

AUTHOR UNKNOWN

NO PRAYERS CAN BE HEARD WHICH DO NOT COME FROM A FORGIVING HEART.

J.C. RYLE

Raising Up a Little Girl...
to Be Forgiving

In every little girl's life there are days when it seems like everything goes wrong. Her little sister rips her favorite skirt. Her best friend says she's found someone she'd rather play with. Her parents promise her a trip to the ice-cream store, but something comes up and the outing is forgotten. Moments like these can do lasting damage to a little girl's heart—unless she cultivates the art of forgiveness.

The first part of forgiveness consists of putting herself in the other person's place—empathy. Little sister didn't know the skirt was so fragile. The best friend may discover she can have more than one very good friend. Mom and Dad needed to attend to something urgent. The little girl's disappointment may be evidenced through her tears, and that's okay. But it's also essential to move on to the next step—forgiveness: "I understand. I'm okay with it. *I forgive you.*"

The skirt will be mended. The friendship will be resumed. The ice cream can be eaten later. And a brand-new day will begin.

Forgiveness is the giving, and so the receiving, of life.

GEORGE MACDONALD

Action springs not
from thought but
from a readiness for
responsibility.

DIETRICH BONHOEFFER

In helping others,
we shall help
ourselves, for
whatever good we
give out completes
the circle and
comes back to us.

FLORA EDWARDS

Never help a child with
a task at which she
feels she can succeed.

MARIA MONTESSORI

Raising Up a Little Girl...
to Be Helpful

Matching up socks from the dryer. Setting silverware in the proper places on the dinner table. Holding the hose while watering the garden. Little ones love to "assist" in any way they can. Yet if parents and caregivers aren't careful, the "I can do it" stage of almost overwhelming enthusiasm to help—often with tasks beyond the little one's skill levels—can turn into a long-lasting stage of "I *won't* do it." The key is finding the balance—working alongside your little girl while gradually adding responsibilities she's capable of handling on her own.

Be prepared to put in the time—*lots* of time—in your daughter's life as she grows. Let her join you as you peel the potatoes. Talk with her as you do laundry: "We fold the clean washcloth in half once, then in half again. Look—it's ready to put on the shelf!" Let her sweep the kitchen floor with her own child-sized broom. And if the result is less than perfect, focus on what she did right. If you're an artist or carpenter, show her how she can create lasting utilitarian and decorative items. Share your hobbies, skills, and talents with her and, at the same time, help her discover her own unique abilities and interests.

A willing helper blesses everyone!

Raising Up a Little Girl...
to Be Patient

"Christmas is in three weeks!"

"Fourteen days till my birthday!"

"Two whole hours until Daddy gets home from work, and then we get to pick up my new bicycle!"

Weeks, days, hours...sometimes even *minutes*! Waiting can be such hard work for a little one. Yet it is in the waiting that the vital seed of patience is sown.

Instead of seeing waiting time as a long, straight homestretch that is the last hurdle until the race is over and the prize is at hand, teach your little girl to view waiting as a series of small challenges with many bends in the road. For instance, when preparing for the holidays, start early and encourage her to help on the little things every day: set out the Nativity scene, bake cookies for the neighbors, cut out paper snowflakes to decorate the windows.

Enlist her help in planning a birthday party. She can frost the cupcakes and twine streamers around the room.

Read a few storybooks together. Encourage her to write stories or draw pictures (how about one of her on her new bicycle?).

Teach your daughter the art of filling waiting time with positive, productive distractions, and she will be well on her way to becoming a patient, peaceful individual.

With time and patience the mulberry leaf becomes a silk gown.

CHINESE PROVERB

The secret of patience...
is to do something else
in the meantime.

AUTHOR UNKNOWN

Adopt the pace of nature:

her secret is patience.

RALPH WALDO EMERSON

ENDURANCE IS NOBLER
THAN STRENGTH, AND
PATIENCE THAN BEAUTY.

JOHN RUSKIN

MODERATION
IS COMMONLY
FIRM, AND
FIRMNESS IS
COMMONLY
SUCCESSFUL.

SAMUEL JOHNSON

Raising Up a Little Girl...
to Be Self-controlled

Little girls find it hard to limit themselves because they find such pleasure in life. And because we live in a culture that doesn't generally practice the art of self-restraint, it sometimes seems unreasonable or unfair to be content with just a little bit. It's challenging to eat just one cookie, to be happy with just one fad toy in a series designed to encourage children to buy more and more.

Yet the failure to practice self-control can result in disastrous consequences. Eating more than is good for us can lead to serious health problems. Putting emphasis on acquiring material possessions can result in financial ruin. Neglecting the needs of others as we focus on our own goals can destroy relationships.

We encourage you to raise up your little girl as one who is able to say *"Stop!"* and mean it. You want a daughter who knows when one is enough, who understands that window-shopping is a pleasure all its own, and who delights in leaving something for tomorrow.

Raising Up a Little Girl...
to Be Imaginative

Little girls can get lost in the world of imagination. *I'm a princess! I'm a flying horse! I'm anything I want to be!* The creativity of a young child is truly something to treasure. That's why we allow our youngsters to head to the grocery store attired in tutus, cowgirl boots, fairy wings, or bunny ears. That's why we supply them with a plethora of art supplies, quality picture books, and mind-strengthening games. That's why we make sure they have unstructured blocks of time to let their imaginations run free.

At some point the world will step in, and the bunny ears and fairy wings will come off. Until then, the key is to maintain a sense of freedom and self during this vital period. You do this by focusing on the process instead of the product. Let the simple things in life move to the foreground. To show your little girl creativity in the kitchen, pick your own strawberries and create scrumptious desserts instead of relying on store-bought goodies. Spend a Saturday morning hunting for thrift store treasures instead of heading for the mall. Help your kids stage a play instead of popping in a DVD.

Raise up your little girl to be secure and confident in who she is and to always hold fast to the precious gift of her imagination.

Happiness lies in the joy of achievement and the thrill of creative effort.

FRANKLIN ROOSEVELT

Imagination is more important than knowledge.

Raising Up a Little Girl...
to Be Dedicated

In recent years research has proven that natural talent alone rarely results in success. Natural talent is wonderful, of course, but it's the hours, days, and years of practice that help a person perfect her skill and reach her goals. Dedication also brings improved performance in all areas of life—scholastic, artistic, athletic, and professional. The ability to stick to a task—to keep working toward the goal—really pays off in the long run.

While a little girl is pursuing her goals and developing the character trait of dedication, she needs healthy doses of encouragement from the grown-ups in her life. Clap for her through each and every soccer game, even if she never makes contact with the ball. During an art time, draw alongside her. Point out how much you love how she fills her entire paper with bright colors—and never let on that you can't tell what she's drawing. When she has a minor bike accident, let her know it's okay to take a break after she crashes, but also communicate that you have faith that she will eventually master riding it (even if *she* has firmly stated she will never, ever ride without training wheels).

By supporting and encouraging your daughter (or grandchild, niece, or friend), you're helping her to understand and appreciate the positive values of hard work, perseverance, and achieving goals.

Few things are impossible
to diligence and skill.

SAMUEL JOHNSON

DOUBTS AND MISTRUST ARE THE MERE
PANIC OF TIMID IMAGINATION, WHICH
THE STEADFAST HEART WILL CONQUER,
AND THE LARGE MIND TRANSCEND.

HELEN KELLER

Diligence is the
mother of good luck,
and God gives all
things to industry.

BENJAMIN FRANKLIN

Raising Up a Little Girl...

to Be Loving and Kind

Fairly early in life, every little girl deals with the pain of being left out. Her best friend chooses someone else as a partner. She's excluded from a birthday party guest list. At playgroup, a few children play the terrible game of ignoring her. Being outside the circle hurts. And it's so tempting for a parent to rush to her little girl's rescue, doing what she can to fix or alleviate the situation. Yet we also know we need to let the little one feel the pain of exclusion so she can learn how to handle negative situations and discover who to turn to for help

Until a person has been left out, she will not know what it feels like to be excluded. And she won't be able to fully understand how to reach out to people who are excluded or don't fit in very well. So instead of stepping in to fix the situation, guide your little girl through the difficult emotions and help her develop kindness and graciousness in her heart.

Encourage her to make more friends. Go over her birthday guest list together, and use this opportunity to see if she's deliberately or subconsciously excluding someone and talk to her about it. Remind her how painful it was when she was excluded, and let her know that ignoring someone isn't acceptable behavior. Fill her cup to overflowing with love and kindness so she has plenty to share with others.

Blessed influence
of one truly loving
soul on another!

GEORGE ELIOT

ANYONE CAN LIVE
SWEETLY, PATIENTLY,
LOVINGLY, PURELY, TILL
THE SUN GOES DOWN.
AND THIS IS ALL LIFE
REALLY MEANS.

ROBERT LOUIS STEVENSON

Kindness is the language
which the deaf can hear
and the blind can see.

MARK TWAIN

Raising Up a Little Girl...
to Be Persistent

"Please let me stay up another hour!"

"I really want to go to the park *right now*!"

"I'm going to keep begging you for this treat until you say yes!"

Do we really need to work on developing the character trait of persistence in young children? Yes—and no. A spirited young girl who never backs down can be intimidating and giving in can seem like less hassle than standing firm. And it's so easy to overlook the positive aspect of her youthful persistence. Think of women who have written their names in the book of history—Helen Keller, Laura Ingalls Wilder, Mother Teresa. Were these women persistent? Absolutely!

In the course of your everyday living, be fair and firm with your young girl. Praise her stick-to-it nature, but calmly and gently let her know when it is time to stop. And always keep your word. When you say, "If you don't stop begging for things, we will leave this toy store immediately, and I will come back alone later to get the birthday present for your friend," follow through if she doesn't stop. Leave the store. Model positive persistence and integrity, and you will teach a young girl how to make an indelible mark on the world.

There is neither encouragement nor room in Bible religion for feeble desires, listless efforts, lazy attitudes; all must be strenuous, urgent, ardent. Flamed desires, impassioned, unwearied insistence delight heaven. God would have His children incorrigibly in earnest and persistently bold in their efforts.

E.M. BOUNDS

LET ME TELL YOU THE SECRET THAT HAS LED ME TO MY GOAL. MY STRENGTH LIES SOLELY IN MY TENACITY.

LOUIS PASTEUR

The secret of success is constancy to purpose.

BENJAMIN FRANKLIN

Raising Up a Little Girl...

to Be Gentle

Does it sound strange that in gentleness there exists unparalleled strength? A gentle heart keeps its temper, doesn't give in to tantrums, and keeps looking ahead in times of trouble. How can we teach young ladies to cultivate hearts of gentleness?

Caring for a pet is a wonderful way to develop a gentle nature—learning the best way to pet a cat, understanding that a bunny needs to be handled carefully, paying attention to the dog so you can tell what it wants or needs. Even the process of taking care of stuffed animals can help guide a child to gentleness.

Taking nature walks around your neighborhood or beyond are fantastic opportunities for learning to respect what God has created and noticing areas of possible involvement, such as picking up litter or clearing weeds.

And for those kids with siblings, there's always room to grow in getting along with them. Teach your daughter that it's not okay to hit or yell at her brother or to take something from her little sister just because she wants it.

Every day there are opportunities to practice gentleness. Help your little girl watch for those moments and then take action. You'll both rejoice in the kind and nurturing soul she is developing.

For attractive lips, speak words of kindness.

AUDREY HEPBURN

Through
wisdom a house
is built, and by
understanding it
is established.

THE BIBLE

WISDOM IS
THE MOST
IMPORTANT
PART OF
HAPPINESS.

SOPHOCLES

Raising Up a Little Girl...
to Be Wise

We tend to think of wisdom in measurable ways. We brag, "My little girl can write her name at the tender age of two." "She's beginning to sound out words at age three." "She can count past one hundred, and she's only four!" While the pursuit of academic-type knowledge is wonderful, overall we need to give our girls the broader gift of wisdom—knowledge in her head, knowledge in her hands, and knowledge in her heart.

One way to teach her to accumulate knowledge and understanding is through reading. Read story after story together, and encourage her as she learns to read. Teach her meaningful hands-on activities, such as finger-knitting with balls of wool, using lacing cards to teach beginning sewing skills, getting seeds to plant to grow gorgeous flowers or vegetables.

Most of all, share with her biblical wisdom that will fill her heart with what is good and true. Help her memorize verses that will nurture her spirit throughout her life. Enjoy getting into God's Word together, and teach her how to pray. Guide her in the way she treats others by modeling a heart of service. Raise up a little girl who will make wise choices.

Knowledge comes, but wisdom lingers.

ALFRED, LORD TENNYSON